God's Healing
for Businesses

*Spiritual principles for unlocking
crisis situations*

David Shadbolt

New Wine Press

New Wine Ministries
PO Box 17
Chichester
West Sussex
United Kingdom
PO19 2AW

ISBN 978-1-905991-04-4

Typeset by CRB Associates, Reepham, Norfolk
Cover design by CCD, www.ccdgroup.co.uk
Printed in Malta

"There are very few people that I can talk to about the complex spiritual issues I face in my business. David is one of those people."
Phil Smith – Entrepreneur

"David is a very practical and spiritual man. His words and leading line up with the Word of God, his care is continuing and his follow-up is sensible. We have always sought to be led by God in our practice's vision, development and daily walk. God has given David to help us."
Martin Steele – Partner, Architectural Practice

"Drawing from the hands-on business experience and proven prophetic insight of its author, this book gives some dynamic keys to seeing the power of God and principles of His Kingdom released into the commercial world. Its innovative message provides tangible and effective keys by which individual enterprises can be turned around into prosperity and effective working practice. It is a much needed step towards seeing afresh God's relevance to the 'real world' and bridging the perceived gap between the Church and the marketplace."
Peter Stott – Team Leader, Portsdown Community Church, Havant

Contents

Foreword

All of life is about creating environments that can attract and keep the presence of God. "On earth as it is in heaven" is the only viable philosophy for every believer to adopt and encourage.

David's book is like the man: real, spiritual and practical. David is a pragmatist. He wants what really works and he will go after it until it does.

If you want a partnership with God that unlocks wealth strategies, enables you to rediscover your spiritual authority so that you can govern in the name of the Lord – and above all else develop effective prayer for your business – then you need the presence of God.

This book charts a course from lack of success to the place of breakthrough. Read it and apply it, and your business will not be the same!

Graham Cooke
Author and speaker

Introduction

Some years ago, a businessman took some time out from his business to seek God. He was determined not to leave this place of prayer until the Lord said something about why his business was not moving forward. As he stilled his heart over the course of those days, into his imagination kept coming a picture. It wasn't at all what he was expecting.

*The picture was of **Jesus** praying*
*for **the business**.*

The thought had never occurred to him that *Jesus* would be praying for a *business*. Church, yes. Ministry, yes. A person, yes. A people group, yes. But a business? As time went on he began to ponder what, exactly, the Lord was praying about. He figured that if it was important enough for the King of kings to bother about, he should know about it too.

While waiting quietly in God's presence there came a growing sense of what the Lord Jesus was actually saying in *His* prayers.

It wasn't about more profit or better clients. It wasn't skilled staff, nor was it a cash injection. In fact, it wasn't any of the obvious business stuff.

Jesus was asking the Father to bring His healing to the business.

At that moment the Lord Jesus touched this man's heart with His fire and invited him to go deeper into His heart and understand His ways more. Gradually, his eyes were opened to better see things the way God does and his ears were opened more to hear what God says. The journey has only just begun and this book is an invitation for those with a similar hunger to join together to rediscover the Father's heart for healing, redemption and restoration in the business world.

It's time to discover a new dimension

Every Christian involved in business is in a truly amazing position. They are seated in Christ in heavenly realms with all the wisdom of God at their disposal. They have the opportunity to demonstrate God's wisdom in the place that they serve.

Often Christians live at the same level as the world, which ignores the realm of the Spirit. The Bible says that spiritual things are discerned by the spiritual man (1 Corinthians 2:12–16). It says we are to transform our thinking by the renewing of our minds (Romans 12:2). In James it says that anyone who lacks wisdom should ask of God and not doubt (James 1:5–8).

As believers we have the most awesome authority and responsibility on the earth. Those who do not know God cannot discern spiritual things (1 Corinthians 2:14), but those who do know God should be able to discern spiritual realities. This we are exhorted to do throughout the New Testament. It is not just for special people or special callings – it is for all believers.

What has this got to do with business?

We need to begin to open our minds and hearts to the fact that even business activities are under the rule of the realm of the Spirit. If we don't we will fight only in our own strength and not rely on God. We will not be able to demonstrate His wisdom, but only a vague Christian ethos about business which has no power behind it. We will suffer from a form of godliness which completely denies its ability to change us and the situations we face in everyday life.

We all walk around a bit like a man who needs glasses. We think we can see OK, until we go for an eye test. It's only then that we realise we need glasses. The

Father is causing many of us to go for an eye test so we realise just how much we need Him to help us understand and walk in the authority that we have been given.

> *"You say, 'I am rich; I have acquired wealth and do not need a thing.' But you do not realise that you are wretched, pitiful, poor, blind and naked. I counsel you to buy from me gold refined in the fire, so that you can become rich; and white clothes to wear, so that you can cover your shameful nakedness; and salve to put on your eyes, so that you can see."*
>
> (Revelation 3:17–18 NIV)

It is only when a test comes that we realise how far short we are falling from His ways. But it is also at that point that God is there with His wisdom – if we will listen.

> *"Give instruction to a wise man and he will be still wiser;*
> *Teach a just man, and he will increase in learning."*
>
> (Proverbs 9:9)

*"Receive my instruction, and not silver,
And knowledge rather than choice gold;
For wisdom is better than rubies,
And all the things one may desire cannot be
compared with her."*

(Proverbs 8:10–11)

*"Hear instruction and be wise,
And do not disdain it."*

(Proverbs 8:33)

Since starting to ask God for keys to unlock and heal businesses, I have learned that time spent with Jesus Christ in prayer brings revelation. Like the disciples in the New Testament, as I spent time with Him, He would constantly stretch me to help me see into the realm of the Spirit. When the disciples encountered a difficult situation, they asked Him how to overcome it. They knew He would always have the answer.

*But His answers were not always what
they would have expected.*

For example, when the disciples found they couldn't cast a demon out, Jesus told them, *"This kind can come out by nothing but prayer **and** fasting"* (see Mark 9:28-29, emphasis added). Another time, Jesus asked Peter to walk on the water towards Him and then he sank. When he asked why, Jesus answered, "You need faith" (see Matthew 14:30–31). When they needed money to pay taxes, Jesus told them to go and find a fish with a coin in its mouth! In this simple, childlike way they grew in Kingdom understanding, wisdom and authority.

Everything in this book has been learned the same way. Facing challenges, crises, seemingly insurmountable situations and asking Jesus how to overcome...

*... waiting before Him to get **His** wisdom, rather than settling for the wisdom of the world.*

This book is deliberately short and to the point. You will not find lengthy Bible exposition, but illustrations and real examples, Scripture references and prayer suggestions. This does not mean that there is not more to say on each subject, but the aim is that you will quickly be able to take practical action. This is how Jesus taught. He is interested in bringing transformation, not just imparting information. We are taught to *do* the word, not just listen to it or read it.

This is very much a "work in progress". We are only just scratching the surface, catching a tiny glimpse of all that God has for us in His amazing Kingdom. As He has taught me in various situations, I have learned some interesting insights into how the spiritual dimension can affect businesses. This book is not meant to be a comprehensive guide to Kingdom business, it is a carefully directed arrow from heaven to help believers overcome when facing specific challenges in business.

There are three areas of healing for business that we will discover together:

- Healing from sinful attitudes
- Healing from spiritual sickness
- Healing from the impact of a curse

To the Western mind, these headings may seem a bit strange. Who equates business with such terms? But God has proven again and again that these are true issues that believers in business need to be aware of and know how to deal with.

God wants to bless the Church and unlock wealth strategies, but as well as being excellent in business management and entrepreneurship, we need to know how to govern in the Spirit or we will be vulnerable. This is why our heavenly Father is showing us how to live in the authority He has given us. Yes, there are practical things we need to understand: team building, good management, cash flow, budgeting, staffing, marketing, product/service development and so on. But we live in a different Kingdom and so there are also *spiritual* things we need to be aware of to bring His Kingdom into our business activities. This goes way beyond character, ethics and sound business

sense. It means seeing all things through spiritual eyes
and hearing all things through spiritual ears – eyes and
ears that have been touched by the Kingdom of our
Lord Jesus.

Even if you are not facing any problems at the
moment, you may in the future and by reading this
book the Holy Spirit will be planting seeds for that
time. At the very least it will encourage you to pray
more for your business and ask God to give you others
in your church or circle of friends who can pray with
you. Pastors and ministers may find this booklet
helpful in equipping their people to go through these
times of testing and growth in God.

Before we start, would you pray with me?

"Father, I thank You that I am seated in heavenly
realms in Jesus Christ because of what He did for
me on the cross. I ask You now to open my eyes
and ears to the spiritual realm. Train me, Lord.
Help me in my weakness and lack of
understanding of Your ways. Make me into what
You want me to be. To know You and be filled
with the fullness of all that You have. I know that
right now creation is groaning and yearning for
the revealing of the sons of God and I am one of
them. I humble myself before You and submit my
mind to You. I ask You to renew my mind to think
more like You. I hand my business back to You.
Thank You for it. Please forgive me if I have

neglected to take care of it spiritually. I speak Your blessing and peace upon it. Surround me with Your love and peace as I read. Let me hide in You and hear Your voice as I read. I bind my mind to Your will. Please protect me from distractions and diversions. Thank You, Lord, You have heard me. You always hear me when I call to You."

Healing from sinful attitudes

God wants to heal our businesses from the ravages of sin and sinful attitudes. It has always been His desire and purpose to redeem **all** things. Do you believe this? Is the peace of God in your business? Do you pray regularly for your business? Are your attitudes hurting your business? God wants us to be channels of blessing. He wants our business to be the same. Sin attacks the *peace* on a business, because the Holy Spirit is in confrontation against the sin. Until the sin is dealt with, the Holy Spirit will continue to address issues. He is a God of peace who is at war with any sin in our lives. He wants the very best for us.

A paraphrase of Psalm 127 done via various translations and a thesaurus brings out the following. I am very grateful for my friend Keith who did this for me.

Unless the Lord, sets up, builds, repairs, makes, establishes your business, family, ministry or home, and unless the Lord hedges it about, guards, protects, attends to, preserves, saves and watches over, it will become to you destructive, a waste, a ruin, idolatry, false, evil, useless and deceptive, it will cause painful toil, hard labour, grievous sorrow, displeasure, anger and false worship.

Or how about Isaiah 48:17–18:

"Thus says the LORD, your Redeemer,
The Holy One of Israel:
'I am the LORD your God,
Who teaches you to profit,
Who leads you by the way you should go.
Oh, that you had heeded My commandments!
Then your peace would have been like a river,
And your righteousness like the waves of the
        sea.'"

Or Proverbs 6:16–19:

"These six things the LORD hates,
Yes, seven are an abomination to Him:
A proud look,
A lying tongue,
Hands that shed innocent blood,
A heart that devises wicked plans,
Feet that are swift in running to evil,
A false witness who speaks lies,
And one who sows discord among brethren."

I started to understand more about what this particular proverb meant following several conversations with a very successful businessman. He had asked me to pray for him and his business as he wanted to go deeper into God and establish businesses that pleased Him. I sensed God was going to start a refiner's fire in this man's life. Purifying, holy fire. I said to him to be absolutely honest with God when conviction came, even in the small things.

Even when it didn't seem to make sense
to his business mind.

Within a couple of weeks he had a meeting with a fellow believer. This believer was causing some trouble in the business and was now costing money. The businessman had decided to get rid of him. The meeting went well in this man's eyes and he used his power and authority to rid the business of this man. Within a couple of days, the businessman couldn't shake off thinking about the meeting. He went before God, as I suggested and was completely honest, and said:

"I keep thinking about that meeting. If there is something that You want to speak to me, it needs to be specific as I personally think it went well. The guy was a menace and had been putting pressure on us."

Immediately he realised that he had lied during the meeting.

Nearly ten times in a half hour meeting.

These lies or "half truths" had forced the other man into a corner. Until then the businessman just thought this was good business sense. He had always done it that way.

But God thought otherwise.

God began to convict him further until he held his hands up humbly before his God and said, "What can I do to make it right?" He then sensed the Holy Spirit telling him to hold another meeting with the man.

> [First item on the agenda]: "Please forgive me for the last meeting." [Second item]: "God has given me authority in this situation. I want to use it to help you get to the place God has for you. I don't think it is working with my company, but let's talk and pray about it. Let's see what God has to say."

It was right that the man leave, as God was calling him to be a missionary, not a businessperson, but God wanted him to leave with blessing, care and honour.

One of the things that the Lord hates is a *"false witness who speaks lies, and one who sows discord among brethren."*

This is **rampant** in Christian business.

I once heard a man saying to another that he didn't trust a certain Christian in business. I asked him whether he had spoken directly to the brother, who I actually knew. He said that he hadn't but he had "heard some things". This is as bad as the world. It's called sin. God hates it. It's one of the six things that we are told He specifically hates. In fact, it is an abomination to Him, the very same word that our Lord uses to describe His feelings for the acts of witchcraft or trying to speak to the dead. Part of the Holy Spirit's job on the earth is to convict us of sin.

He is not *just* there to make us feel good or have goose bumps in church meetings.

Another businessman I spent time with did the complete opposite. When the conviction of God started to come upon him, he covered up and ran from God. The first time I met him I knew that God's fire was coming. But his response was to continue in unrighteousness.

He wouldn't let God touch the hurts and wounds that were causing him to have such problems.

Despite pleadings and warnings from friends, and offers of ministry for healing in his life, he eventually lost his business. God still loves him and he is still called by God to do great things for Him in business, but there needs to be a season of humbling, repentance and most importantly, healing, before God raises him up again.

The sad thing is that this man was being heralded as a role model to other believers, because he moved in the spiritual gifts and said the right things. But God saw the secrets of his heart. Interestingly, this man also talked a lot about how much money his business could make for God.

But if God is not in the getting of it,
He is not in the owning of it.

We must be people who have confidence to boldly approach our heavenly Father no matter what the state of our soul is or what mistakes we have made (Hebrews 4:5–16). Run *to* God when He starts to show you things that He wants to change, don't run away from Him. When we run to Him, He has wide open arms *and* transforming power (Hebrews 12:6–11).

There are many ways of thinking and behaving that may indicate an underlying heart attitude that the Holy Spirit would like to speak to us about. Here are just a few thoughts to consider. You may find these a helpful guide as you speak to Him about your business.

1. **Do you respect your customers?** Or in your thinking are they just gullible enough to buy your product/ service? God loves them just as much as He loves you. Are you just using them to achieve *your* goals?
2. **Do you believe in and facilitate every member of staff to achieve their potential within your organisation?** Are you doing everything possible to make that happen? If you don't are you willing to help them into a new place?

3. Are you doing everything possible to reduce your debt burden? Or are you just putting your trust in bank loans and credit?

4. Do you lie, exaggerate or make any knowingly false claims in any of your company literature? Do you falsely criticise others in any communication?

5. Do routine business demands encourage or lead to the break-up of important relationships and families? Are long hours constantly taking their toll on you and your company's staff? Are the frequent breakfast meetings and after work dinners absolutely necessary? Do they lead to an unspoken ethos of extended work hours?

6. Are you willing to shut the business down, sell it or hand it to another to run, if you don't really believe in your heart of hearts that this is your destiny? People sometimes start businesses on the rebound from hurtful situations. Generally this is not a solid foundation for a long-term business. It can result in much grief. God can redeem it, but it may be that you are in the wrong place.

7. Has your company lost the human touch? Are you so busy with business, goals and deadlines that you've lost touch with the humanity you deal with every day? The humanity for which Jesus left the glory of heaven, came to earth and then died on the cross?

8. **Does your company actively encourage customers to borrow beyond their ability to repay? Does your company use unscrupulous methods of debt collection?**

9. **Are you wasting money that you have borrowed or had invested in your company?** Companies can be doing well and sometimes investment, instead of helping, can bring a spirit of destruction because it diverts from God's chosen path.

10. **How are things at home?** We are complete people, God does not divide different aspects of our life into separate boxes. Your attitude at home or church could be adversely affecting your business.

People make businesses. People in authority in the business need to be walking with God to protect the business from sin. If you don't, who will?

Just like a believer can *choose* to introduce evil into their life, a redeemed businessperson can introduce evil into their business through ignorance and lack of clear biblical teaching. God wants to use our businesses to be outposts of His love and demonstrations of His ways in this crazy mixed up, and often scared, world.

For example, having your focus *only* on profit is not honouring God. It's a bit like saying the only reason we are on earth is to have sex. Yes, it's needed to keep the world going. Yes, it's part His plan for our lives, within the framework of marriage. But thinking it is the only reason for our existence on the earth is unbalanced thinking and leads to problems.

When God breathed into your business and gave it life, He had more in His heart than a money making machine, in the same way that when He breathed life into you He saw much more than a procreation machine.

God sees who your business is going to touch. He knows how it is going to transform lives. We have not often been taught this in the Church and so we are easy prey to the spirits of mammon, greed and envy. God is waiting with open arms to forgive you and heal you and your business of the ravages of sin. God wants your business to so reflect His heart that people will feel His love through it. He wants to give you plans from heaven to grow the fruit of the Spirit in your office, alongside your plans for financial growth. There must also be a readiness to accept correction where it is necessary and a determination to demonstrate the reality of redemption. Sincere repentance, making apology where it is due, honours God and will speak volumes to those you come into contact with.

A few tips have helped people in this process.

1. **Find ways of discovering your blind spots.**
   If you have one, make sure you involve your spouse (husband/wife) in every major business decision. If no spouse, then ask a good friend of the opposite sex, as they often see things that we

don't and can expose our blind spots. Ask God to
give them discernment beyond their business
knowledge.

2. **Become accountable.** Do what you can to gather
   a group of believers – excluding non-executive
   directors and fellow directors – that you are
   accountable to for the running of the business as
   well as other areas of your life. Open your business
   and the attitudes in the business to their scrutiny. In
   the Body of Christ we should never be on our own.

3. **Enlist regular prayer support.** Ask God to give
   you some prayerful people who can *visit* your
   business every few months and spend time
   waiting on God on location to see what He may
   be saying. Make this event as un-missable as the
   board meeting or a meeting with the bank
   manager. You will be amazed by what God will
   do as you seek Him.

God's Kingdom, God's government, is upside-down
to the world's. He rules by serving, not snatching or
grabbing. The enemy wants to rob you of your dignity
and rest in Jesus. These practical tips can help to
protect you and increase the peace in your business.
This in turn will mean that everyone who touches
your business will begin to touch the peace and
presence of Jesus. They will notice the difference
and opportunities will open up for you to share
about Him.

Having read this, you may like to pray the following prayer:

"Father, thank You for Your love and revelation. Where things are not right in Your eyes, help me to work with You to put them right. Please forgive me for the times that I have allowed things into my business and business activities which are not helpful. Forgive me for dishonouring You. Thank You for the cleansing power of the blood of the Lord Jesus Christ. Please give me strategy and plans for the spiritual health of my business as well as its practical outworking. Amen."

Healing from spiritual sickness

A sick business is one where its **effectiveness** is under attack. If you are sick, you don't function as well as you should and could. It could be a cold or headache, in which case you can still carry on, it's just more painful and slightly slower. Or it could be something more serious which requires surgery or extended times of rest. Sometimes we get sick because we don't look after ourselves properly. At others it's because there are "bugs" in the air.

In the same way, there can be different levels of sickness within a business. It could be that you have neglected certain aspects. Now you are reaping what you sowed. I don't say this to condemn you but to cause you to turn to the Father for wisdom and help in your time of need. He is always there for you.

> "Let us therefore come boldly to the throne of
> grace, that we may obtain mercy and find
> grace to help in time of need."
>
> (Hebrews 4:16)

Let God speak to you. He may speak directly or He may
speak through others. He has been around a lot longer
than you and can help you understand things that have
gone wrong.

> "Counsel is mine, and sound wisdom;
> I am understanding, I have strength."
>
> (Proverbs 8:14)

Often there will be very practical things that need to
be adjusted when it is a sick business. Bill Hamon, a
mature and reputable prophet, once got all the business
people in a church to come forward in a meeting.
In his book, *Prophets and Personal Prophecy*, he tells
the story:

> "...the Lord revealed to me that there were
> many men in that service who owned their own
> businesses but that they were at a standstill. He
> told me there was a particular problem in each

business that was the key hindrance ... To each
one God spoke something different. To one He
talked about problems in his accounting
department; to another his need to cut back
personnel and regroup and re-evaluate; to another
to expand into other fields. The prophetic word
told one man that God had been dealing with him
for years about imbalance in his life between
business and family and that He was not going to
bless his business any more until he put things in
order." [1]

Does it surprise you that God would speak about very
practical things in our businesses? It was a surprise to
Simon Peter when Jesus borrowed his boat to preach
to a crowd and, when He had finished speaking, then
turned His attention to Peter's need – to catch fish to
sell. Jesus had not forgotten Simon's business need,
it was as valid as the crowd's need for spiritual
nourishment. Jesus told Peter to put his net out again
when he had fished all night and caught nothing,
and he caught so many fish that he needed help from
the other disciples to gather the catch. God directed
him to where the fish were (Luke 5:1–9). God can
supernaturally direct us today to make adjustments in
very practical ways to help our businesses become
more effective. He really does love us this much.

1. Bill Hamon, *Prophets and Personal Prophecy*, Destiny Image,
    1987.

Someone I know had some prayerful people come to his business and pray. As they prayed together, God started to give impressions to one of the visitors. God was showing them that a previous business that had rented this same office had failed and that an influence of hopelessness and defeat from the past needed to be prayed off. Later the owner of the business did some research and found out that it was true. When they prayed about this specific issue, the office atmosphere grew in hope and faith for the future. Another person felt that there was an evil influence rooted in the business, but based in another part of the world and then named the actual region. Again, this was true. The owner of the business was indeed dealing with a very difficult and challenging personnel situation in another region of the world. This confirmation from God, actually labelling the activity as "evil", gave the directors the courage to carry out some major changes and procrastinate no longer.

On the way to one business I had been invited to pray for, I had the sense from the Holy Spirit that the authority of the Managing Director was being undermined. It was a small business with just a few staff, so it should be an easy problem to fix. As I shared this with the boss, at first he couldn't make sense of it. It was a fledgling business but relations with the staff were good. Relations with the few clients they had were healthy. Yet God was clearly saying to me that this man's authority was being undermined.

As we prayed he suddenly remembered about the man who ran the business in the next door office. He had started a rival company offering the same service as the man I was praying for. Each time they met, this man's office neighbour boasted of new contracts won. "I felt so small after each conversation. Sometimes he even came into my office to tell me!" We prayed and asked God to remove any influence this neighbour's words may have had. Immediately the peace of God came into the office. And wisdom came to the Managing Director regarding how to deal with his neighbour, who was also a believer!

The thing is that businesses are complex, incredibly varied and there can be many, many issues which cannot be covered in this small book, but God knows and God can speak to us if we are open to His wisdom and care. One word from God can contain more than all the management books put together. At least once we have the word of direction or insight we know which books to read to put it right!

In my own business we were once going through a rough time. As I prayed about the situation God showed me that we had taken on a certain (very well paying) client when He had told me not to.

God said, "David, you knew in your heart I was telling you not to, but you yielded to peer pressure and financial need. You need to repent, finish the project you are working on and then resign the account with grace and dignity."

I obeyed and things started to get right in my company. However, we had forfeited other work which we would have been able to do, had we not been so busy with this one client. Morale had also been dented because this client had been very difficult to work with. We needed some time to recover and recuperate from this too.

It may be that you have taken on a business, or invested in one and there are problems arising that you knew nothing about when you made the decision to take it on. I challenge you, just for a moment, to put aside your business mind (and maybe your anger) and ask God to show you what's going on.

I was asked for advice by someone who had been asked to pray for a business that a friend was in the process of buying. Immediately into my spirit came three things. First, there was a freemason link which needed to be broken. Second, although I didn't know what the business was, there were overseas connections that had brought unhelpful influences. These needed to be cut off too. Third, this could only be done once the transfer of authority had been completed. Once the man had taken ownership of the business, he could pray those prayers and God would sort out the issues. It turned out that the company was an import business supplying goods to a UK city where heavy freemasonry "backhanders" and "favours" are the norm. He was about to take on a sick business, but in His mercy God spoke to him and pointed out it needed healing first.

Another time I was sitting at home reading a book, when I "saw" that the computer systems of one of the businesses I regularly pray for was going to come under virus attack. Immediately I rang the company to make sure they had the very latest virus software installed. As soon as I told them, they laughed. "We are just downloading the very latest patches now!" God was confirming to me that He was speaking. The systems were never harmed as the proper protection was put in place. Who knows what disaster had been averted by our joint obedience to the prompting of the Holy Spirit in this way?

Sometimes, the delay in receiving answered prayer or the things that seem to hinder us in business are actually the Lord slowing things down or withholding because He wants to get our attention and do things in our hearts or change our circumstances. He knows what foundations are needed in heart and relationship. And He knows the connections we are going to need to achieve all that is in His heart for our business. There can be times when it seems He is standing in our way. I have seen this happen many times when the business person's relationship with his or her church is poor. It is very, very, easy to develop an independent attitude when we become successful, so sometimes the Lord Jesus ensures we have strong relationships with other Christians in place before He gives us the success He is promising. It could also be that you have tried to move too fast and have run ahead of the Lord. If the enemy can't stop you, he will get behind you and push you too fast. Both are just as bad and damaging in the Kingdom of God.

I was coaching a senior manager who had a passion to change the heart of the global business he worked for. Our aim in spending time together was to help him hear the voice of the Lord more clearly for himself. He had incredible vision and had achieved so much in the short time he had been there and was keen to keep moving ahead. He certainly had the ability and the favour from his peers throughout the corporation. However, I sensed a check from the Lord. God said, "Tell him I need to rearrange some things before he can move ahead with the things on his heart. Nothing much is going to happen in the next six months. It's a time of consolidation. Don't expect or force anything major to happen." As we spoke about it I could see that this "action man" was going to find it difficult to wait. Within two weeks, God, in His amazing kindness and attention to detail, gave someone on the opposite side of the world, who this man had not met before, exactly the same instruction to pass on! Maybe you have been so fed on faith and action teaching that you don't understand God's timing and you have moved ahead of the Lord and the business is suffering for it now.

Until now, believing business people have managed to thrive and develop businesses without necessarily having guidance and insight from the Holy Spirit. But as God raises His people to take more ground from the enemy in the world of commerce, the enemy is hitting back harder. We need greater supernatural assistance from our heavenly Father to make our businesses prosper, thrive and stay healthy. Sometimes the supernatural assistance we receive will be words of practical direction and adjustment.

Maybe you would like to pray the following prayer:

"Father, I didn't realise that You knew so much about business! Help me to listen to Your voice. You know if there is any sickness affecting my business. I ask You to walk through every aspect of my business by Your Spirit and bring to my attention and the attention of those around me what You find. Help me to be more open to Your promptings and to see things the way You see them. I ask You to bring Your healing balm to aspects of my business that You see are sick and help me to learn how to properly look after those areas in the future. Thank You that You hear me when I call out to You."

Healing from the impact of a curse

This is probably the most surprising of all the aspects that God has revealed to me. A curse, in business terms, is an attempt to *stagnate* or *immobilise* it, which is deadly in terms of cash flow and growth. At first, I really couldn't believe that businesses run by believers could be cursed by the enemy. Surely, in His love, God would not allow this to happen? When God started showing me this revelation, I asked Him for confirmation and found myself reading Deuteronomy 28, Malachi 4:5–6 and where Jesus cursed the fig tree in Mark 11:12–14, 20–24.

He started to show me that my current understanding of the word "curse" was very narrow and this was leading me to misunderstand His ways and the workings of the spiritual realm. I had been a believer for seventeen years, but it was as though there were still roadblocks in my mind that would not let me take hold of this particular truth and allow it to integrate fully into my thought processes. As I mulled it over, one day it seemed quite plausible to me, but the next it would seem quite unreal. So the process continued to alternate for several weeks. Maybe you face the same challenge that I did. I urge you to persevere in seeking His face.

> "*I beseech you* [urge you strongly] *therefore, brethren, by the mercies of God, that you present your bodies a living sacrifice, holy, acceptable to God, which is your reasonable service. And do not be conformed to this world, but be transformed by the renewing of your mind, that you may prove what is that good and acceptable and perfect will of God.*"
>
> (Romans 12:1–2)

It is so worth it. But you may find you have to contend for the ground against the enemy who really, really doesn't want you to get hold of it.

As I continued to seek the Lord over the months, I began to realise that the enemy has been pretty smart at fooling many of us over this issue. I think it's about time this trick was exposed for the sham that it is.

I suggest that our enemy has fooled us by means of the following ways of thinking:

1. Making us think that curses can only come if we are being specifically attacked by a witches' coven. Many Christians, if you mention the word "curse", immediately imagine a midnight coven convention muttering curses over the area.
2. Making us frightened to speak the word "curse" itself because of what people might think, i.e. being labelled a "weirdo". Jesus didn't seem to mind using the word when He was on earth.
3. Making us think that curses are rare. Therefore if we *are* affected we must be a special case. Nobody wants to be special for *that* reason!
4. Making us think that curses are something to be scared of. Again meaning we don't consider them.
5. Making us think that any understanding of curses is only for those in "full-time" ministry or those directly involved in deliverance – a Christian kind of polite sweeping under the carpet.
6. Making us think that it is such an awful, sinful and despicable thing to even admit to the possibility of being under a curse that we don't even mention the word.

For these reasons, and probably others too, we tend not to welcome this word into our vocabulary or understanding. If any of these six attitudes reflect your current thinking, would you start to ask God to open your heart to the possibility that you may be wrong?

Can you see what a trap the enemy has laid? God

has, through His Son Jesus Christ dying on the cross, given us provision for a commonly found situation – a curse. One which He knows still operates on the earth and one which He wants to teach us to understand, know how to deal with, and not suffer from. The enemy, knowing the power that this knowledge brings against him, has so diverted our attention that we do not think to use the provision God Himself has made for us. This means that the enemy can work openly under our nose without us even being aware of it or even wanting to face up to the possibility.

I had to face these issues as God started to show me that my thinking was wrong and it needed to change if I was to grow in Kingdom understanding and authority. I asked God to forgive me for my trust in my own strength and wisdom. Then I asked Him to renew my mind in this area as I read His Word, the Bible.

I am very pleased to say that this does not now mean that everywhere I go I see or sense a curse, but this truth now forms an important part of my "toolset" when I am meeting with, praying with/for or coaching believing business people in the ways of the Holy Spirit. It's just one "tool" in the same way that a management consultant would have "tips for dealing with awkward staff" as one tool in his or her toolset for solving personnel issues. If God speaks into my spirit about a curse operating in a particular situation, I don't freak out, start to speak in hushed tones or think that this must be a special, "rare" case. At the same time, now I am open to this truth, He is continuing to teach me ways to recognise symptoms, causes and learn different ways to overcome. Our God wants us to work with Him to destroy all the enemy's works.

What have I learned? Some of the symptoms of a cursed business, or one that has had specific assignments from the enemy against it, are as follows. This is not an exhaustive list, but there are certain characteristics that seem to always be there. The main common denominator appears to be that even when everything seems to be in order, the business starts to stagnate. Somehow, progress is immobilised and there are distractions which take the business away from its central focus. The market is right, the product is right, the people are right, but somehow it is as though there is a dark cloud which hangs around that you cannot break through.

Some specific symptoms that could well be caused by a curse are listed below. My limited experience so far indicates that normally there will be several evident if a curse is in fact in operation.

1. Even though good, dependable, work is being done, there is no repeat business.
2. A sudden, unexplainable, increase of bad debts.
3. Attack on reputation for no apparent or justifiable reason, often from a loyal source.
4. Sustained sickness on key members of staff.
5. Constant questioning of motives and ability.

6. Accidents in cars or when travelling on business.
7. Confusion and misunderstanding, inside the company and among clients. This is not just because of poor communication, which can be fixed by better dialogue.
8. Profits being eroded by a series of "bizarre" or "unusual" things happening which cost money and time which had not been budgeted for.
9. Consistent delays in contracts. (One business we prayed for to break this off it received calls the very next day from the people who had been delaying for months on contracts.)

As you can see, these are all things that come at us over which we seem to have **no control.** In fact, one of the phrases I have often heard when talking to highly skilled and experienced business people who are facing this issue has been, "I've gone through everything but just can't work out what I'm doing wrong." This then brings the focus back to them, which can often bring condemnation and a horrible sense of failure, and with it, hopelessness. The master deception from the enemy is that the problem lies with us, so that we resign ourselves to it, say, "That's life", and struggle on.

We must not begin seeing curses everywhere we turn, as this is unhelpful and untrue. But God is far bigger than anything the enemy can throw at us, and the Lord does want our eyes opened to realise that it is possible to be affected. He also wants us to know how to deal with it if it arises. If your business is suffering from several of the above symptoms, then it may well be the subject of a curse.

We know from former Satanists that Satanists pray against Christian churches, homes, families and businesses. We also know that other faiths, particularly from other parts of the world understand the spiritual realm much better than most Western Christians and can take advantage of our ignorance. God further underlined the importance of this issue to me recently, because as I was writing this section of the book, a UK businessman told me of a time when he and his colleagues had been cursed by a person of another faith who felt he had been let down by them. Because they had let him down, he said he was going to curse them to make their lives a misery. Almost immediately, all sorts of strange things started happening. Fortunately, the man I spoke to was a member of a church that understood spiritual things and the curse was quickly broken off him, but not before his car had been involved in a crash. Unfortunately, his colleagues were not so lucky and one ended up becoming very ill.

I was talking to some young Ugandans who told me a similar story. There had been a businesswoman in their church who could not sell some of her land. The price was right, the location was ideal and lots of people had visited to see it. But nobody had bought the land. She had got so fed up with this that she asked the last potential buyer who visited why they wouldn't buy it. Was it the price? Was it the location? What was wrong? How could they come to some deal? This person replied, "As soon as I walked on the land I heard a voice saying to me 'If you buy this land you will suffer harm.'" The lady went straight to her church leaders. They discerned a curse was operating and, after time fasting and seeking the Lord, broke it in the name of Jesus. The last visitor was invited back again. This time he heard nothing and bought at the original price. Later they found out that a witchdoctor had actually been paid by a business rival to curse this businesswoman's land.

Now picture this in a Western world scenario. As business people, we are sometimes so dull in our spiritual senses. God wants to help us grow in this area. He wants us to walk in much more wisdom of spiritual realities than we currently do. Then we will see more of God's power released in our businesses than we could possibly imagine.

A curse can also be a result of our own behaviour or speech. This is difficult for us to hear. If this *is* the case, I believe that as we pray God will show us. While fasting and praying, begin to ask God if there is anything that you may need to put right. Scripture says *"A curse without cause shall not alight"* (Proverbs 26:2). Examine your conscience before God and ask the Holy Spirit to show you anything specific you need to deal with.

Have you sacked someone without justification? Have you been dishonest on your tax return? Have you charged a client more hours than you actually did? Or made someone "redundant" when you knew that you would refill the very same post as soon as they went? Have you repeatedly and consistently spoken negatively over your business, your staff, your clients, particular projects or any of the equipment you use?

In the Old Testament there is a story of a king who was so fearful of the people of Israel he hired a prophet to curse them. This wicked king knew that a curse spoken by one man with God behind him could bring defeat to a whole nation (see Numbers 22:1–25; 31:16). Do we realise that now we are in Christ, our words are incredibly powerful too? We can bring heaven or bring hell by our words.

In the book of James, it tells us to keep a tight rein on our tongue and warns of the consequences if we don't.

> *"If anyone considers himself religious and yet does not keep a tight rein on his tongue, he deceives himself and his religion is worthless."*
>
> (James 1:26 NIV)

> *"The tongue also is a fire, a world of evil among the parts of the body. It corrupts the*

> *whole person, sets the whole course of his*
> *life on fire, and is itself set on fire by hell. All*
> *kinds of animals, birds, reptiles and creatures*
> *of the sea are being tamed and have been*
> *tamed by man, but no man can tame the*
> *tongue. It is a restless evil, full of deadly*
> *poison. With the tongue we praise our Lord*
> *and Father, and with it we curse men, who*
> *have been made in God's likeness. Out of the*
> *same mouth come praise and cursing. My*
> *brothers, this should not be."*
>
> (James 3:6–10 NIV)

I received a call from a businessman one day who was having tremendous problems with a project which was dragging on and on. There seemed to be no end to it. Despite all their efforts, it was not moving forwards. It was losing money and detracting from other work. After discussing the issue and praying together, I led him in a prayer of repentance for all the negative words that had been spoken over the project, by him and those working on his behalf. He then asked God to forgive him for his attitude towards the client and his staff.

Together we then spoke blessing and favour over the project, staff and client in the name of Jesus Christ. I then suggested he should spend the evening in the office on his own seeking God and worshipping Him.

"Ask God to give you faith to really believe that He knows how to solve this problem. Maybe, in His kindness, He will now supernaturally give you keys to unlock this project." The following morning, during a meeting with one of his programmers, the following happened. These are his words: "At one point in the conversation, it felt like I was speaking in tongues, because I wasn't using my mind and the presence of God was suddenly there. In that moment, the questions I asked the programmer unlocked the vital parts of the project that were causing so many problems."

A manager rang me who was having big problems with a member of staff. They were about to have a telephone conference which my friend was dreading, so I asked if she was able to go somewhere privately right then and speak in tongues until God spoke to her. Later when we spoke again she told me that God had said, "Stop using your mouth to curse, instead use it to bless. Your own words have blocked Me from answering your prayers for help." She began to bless the person in the name of Jesus and from that moment the relationship radically improved. Who knows what that blessing did in the life of the member of staff? Maybe they had been criticised all their life and nobody had ever spoken *life* and *blessing* over them. Maybe that was the root of many of their problems. Maybe demons that had been tormenting them for years and affecting the whole atmosphere of the business had been commanded to leave as a result of this blessing. We will only know in eternity, but at that moment, my friend stepped into the authority she has as a believer and, as promised in the Bible, heaven responded.

These are only a few examples to illustrate how our *own* words and attitudes can not only curse aspects of our business but also block us from receiving supernatural help from our loving heavenly Father. God wants us to understand the power of our words. We must learn to speak *life* into every situation we find ourselves in, even if they are not pleasing to us or are giving us problems. Then God can act on our behalf. And even if, in His wisdom, He chooses not to intervene right then, at least we have not used our tongues to curse, which God our Father strongly encourages us *not* to do!

All these types of things could well be entry points for the enemy which are affecting the running of your business. They need to be identified and shut down. Believe that your heavenly Father will reveal to you if there are such entry points. It's good if during this time you gather others to pray with you through any issues that arise. If something comes to mind, pray it through. His desire is to release movement and life back into the business.

In my experience, we don't always need to dig around for a long time to find out the source of the problem. If God wants us to put something specific right, He will speak to us in detail as we seek His face.

That is the job of the Holy Spirit, to take that which is from Jesus and make it known to us. Then we can stand in the authority that we have been given in Christ Jesus to see them broken off. And we can continue to stand and help others to stand if we see similar things occurring elsewhere in the Body of Christ. We can thank our heavenly Father that in His redemptive power He has made a way through each impasse that seems impossible for us to see.

If after reading this section you think that your business or an aspect of your business might be suffering from the impact of a curse it is very important to be thankful to God for everything He is and does. If your eyes are being opened to the spiritual realm, don't get tricked into only seeing the enemy. Ungratefulness, a "why me?" attitude or a focus on the enemy will not cause faith to grow in your heart. Don't go straight into battle without acknowledging Christ's supremacy, majesty, holiness and kingship. In *all* of creation, King Jesus is the most exalted, except for the Father Himself. Even the most glorious and powerful angelic majesties bow down in honour to Him. All authority in heaven and earth has been given to Him. There is no president or king or business leader who has ever come close to the glory or majesty of our King.

The most remarkable thing of all is that we are not just called to be His subjects, but actual members of His Body – His very Person! This battle belongs to the

Lord, although He may use your voice to commence it, in the same way that in your body the brain or mind decides on an arm movement, but the arm has to make the actual move.

So it is in the Kingdom. The head, that is Christ, gives us, His Body on earth, instructions which we need to carry out to see the task completed. It is helpful if you are able to spend some time fasting to help you better focus on the Lord during this time. Fasting helps to tune us into spiritual things. There are plenty of books on fasting and I cannot cover the issue in this short book, but you can ask your pastor or minister for some advice regarding fasting if you have any questions about it.

Although you should not be scared, it is also very important that you do not treat spiritual things lightly. You should remember that you are standing on the earth against demonic forces which, without God, we have absolutely no hope against. The enemy has been around a lot longer than you and has been causing problems for many thousands of years. He plays dirty. And he knows the rules better than we do. But we have God on our side, if we know Him and if we humble ourselves before Him. Remember, He gives grace to the humble, but *He* (that is God Himself) opposes the proud. In spiritual warfare we must fight from a place of humility and submission to Jesus Christ, not having a "gung-ho" attitude which stems from arrogance and pride. Business people, who are generally used to being able to control situations through their own skills, resources and cleverness, particularly, need to be aware of this.

*At this point, your bank account, your contacts, your market share, your cleverness and your staff are of **no benefit** whatsoever.*

Only your trust in the power and faithfulness of the Lord Jesus Christ and the power He has put into your mouth.

A prayer:

"Father, I come before You and humble myself. I thank You that You have won the victory in Christ Jesus. Thank You for preparing me for this time of spiritual warfare. Thank You for forgiving all my sin by dying on the cross and clothing me in Your righteousness. I have done all that I can do and I have put right everything that You have spoken to me about. Now I look to You, Lord, to break any assignment from the enemy against my business. I stand in the name of the Lord Jesus Christ and in the full armour that He has provided and cut off any curse that has come upon my business through my own fault or through the actions or words of others against it. I declare it has no right to be here and I ask You to bring Your peace upon my business and everything and everyone associated with it. Still this storm, Lord. I speak blessing and peace over my business, its staff [*name each one in turn if you can*], its network of contacts [*again, name in turn as many as you can*] and all its transactions [*name specifics if possible*]. I thank You for it in Jesus' name. Thank You that You have set it free to be everything You have purposed it to be. I ask You in Your mercy to restore all money, time and anything else the enemy has stolen during this time of attack."

Conclusion

For many of you reading this, it's time to study the scriptures mentioned, meditate on them, pray the prayers and start to see change for the better. You may want to write your own prayers that are specific to your own situation. Keep praying until you start to hear the Lord's answers. Then bring the understanding that He gives together with your own experience and knowledge of how your business ticks. I am certainly not saying that all businesses facing problems fall into one of these categories. Even if the problem is bad management, ineffective marketing, lousy product or one of many other known practical business issues, God can highlight which ones you need to focus on.

I hope that these few insights have increased your own spiritual "toolset" for determining the solution to everyday practical problems you may face. At the very least I hope it inspires you to pray more for your business and encourage others you know to pray for businesses and business people too. If this book results in every business receiving increased prayer around it, then it will have achieved its purpose.

If you are not in relationship with a local church or body of believers, may I encourage you to find one and develop healthy friendships as an absolute priority. Being in business is a spiritual battle and your heavenly Father knows that fighting on your own will eventually exhaust you, harden your heart and weaken your resolve against the enemy's onslaught. Church leaders who are open to the supernatural working of God, will, in the coming years, increasingly be given wisdom and insight for business people to walk through some of these issues outlined. So ask God to lead you to them now.

One more thing: as I begin to speak to people on the subject of curses, one question that keeps being asked is, "Could this be what is stopping my new business idea work?" All I can say is that at this stage in my journey with the Holy Spirit, I have not seen or been informed by the Lord that a curse operating has *prevented* a new business get off the ground. Instead I would be asking them about their sales strategy – is there one? Are they even making the calls? Do they know how to? Are they doing what they can to make contact with potential clients? Have they thought carefully about the way they are presenting their business to others? Do they need to learn basic business skills? Have they rushed ahead of the Lord's timing? Maybe some more practical learning is needed first.

For example, the Lord first spoke to me about having a business eleven years before it actually happened and in those years I had several opportunities to take that route, but each time the Holy Spirit said, "Not yet." I used those years to prepare for that moment and when it finally started, everything was in place and it just took off. I would be encouraging the person to pray for the Lord's favour and timing in their life and asking God to lead them to where He wants them to be. I would also be asking them if they had received clear direction from the Lord to start the business in the first place. If they believed they had, how did He speak to them? Was it confirmed by others? It might sound strong, but the consequences of launching out without our Father's instructions are so awful that I wouldn't want anyone to put themselves in that position.

If anyone reading is in a start-up situation as either self-employed, small business or freelance, they may find that the motivational booklet *Better Money Management for the Self Employed* co-written with Keith Tondeur and published by Credit Action (www.creditaction.com) has some useful suggestions to think about. There are plenty of other books, courses, online websites and correspondence schools available to get your basic business skills in place, if that is what you need right now. Learndirect is one of them. It is also probably worth talking to your local government office to get a list of local places and organisations that can provide that kind of help. Soon, God will ensure that such basic teaching will be available through churches, ministries and Christian Business Schools, but we are not quite there yet, so meanwhile use all that is on offer in the world.

I pray that the same God who led Moses and king David will lead you as you seek to build a business that honours Him and becomes a place of His wisdom, presence and love in this troubled world.

About the author

David Shadbolt is an author and business advisor with a difference. The difference is that he focuses primarily on spiritual issues affecting businesses, of which the owners or board members are often completely unaware. Insights that come from this sharp focus have helped many businesses. They have also given an increased sense of purpose and destiny to those running the businesses. David travels widely and loves to help entrepreneurs, company directors, boards, investors and organisations to discover and explore further how the invisible affects the visible.

David also travels itinerantly working with organisations and leaders of churches who desire their congregations to come into a greater awareness of the God who speaks and the God who longs to demonstrate the supernatural power of the Kingdom.

David's home base is with his wife and son in England. For more information visit his website at: www.davidshadbolt.com

We hope you enjoyed reading this New Wine book.
For details of other New Wine books
and a range of 2,000 titles from other
Word and Spirit publishers visit our website:
www.newwineministries.co.uk